DAD,
YOU
STAND
TALL

BONNIE
LOUISE
KUCHLER

Andrews McMeel
Publishing
Kansas City

06 07 08 09 10 SDB 10 9 8 7 6 5 4 3 2 1

ISBN-13: 978-0-7407-5812-6
ISBN-10: 0-7407-5812-8

Library of Congress Control Number: 2005936487

Design by Pete Lippincott

In memory of my dad.

Each year since his passing,
he's grown taller in
my memories.

ACKNOWLEDGMENTS

*Thanks to my editor,
Chris Schillig, and
the many others at
Andrews McMeel
who molded this book
out of my simple words.*

*And thanks to
the photographers
whose stirring images
breathed life into
those words.*

Dad, from
your vantage point

you see a life
I have yet to know.

Thanks for the times
you've let me look at the
world from your shoulders.

B y watching you I've learned so much.

Without words
you've taught me about
strength and integrity.

You've taught me that
strength often means

bending and
"rolling with the punches,"

while integrity means

unmasked honesty.

You've given me the
confidence to be myself

and to follow my own path.

Dad, you stand tall.

You've encouraged me to
grow and find success

wherever I am,
with whatever I have.

You've pushed me to reach for the stars

and not settle for less than the sky.

You've taught me that
by cutting back,

*I can be
more productive,*

*and you've shown me that
sometimes the best
thing I can do*

*is stand still and
enjoy the moment
while the world rushes by.*

You've weathered a lot of storms in your life,

and you've reminded me that dark days will pass.

The sun
will shine again.

Spring will return.

I *respect*

all you've gone through

*to become
who you are today.*

These things make you a landmark.

And a survivor.

Dad, you stand tall.

Throughout my life
I've relied on you
in one way
or another

and enjoyed
the comfort of it.

There's a solidness
about you
that makes me
feel secure.

I know where to run
when I'm afraid,

*and you wisely point
me in the right
direction.*

Y ou've always given me
a soft place to land . . .

a home.

You let me hang on to
you until I was
ready to let go . . .

to face the world, and my

battles, on my own.

My life
wouldn't be the same
without you.

Dad, you stand tall.

Y ou've put up with a lot

from me over the years.

A nd from
others . . .

I've always expected
you to be there
when I needed you,

and you always were.

So often
I've taken you for granted.

It took me
a long time to
appreciate the sacrifices
you've made, to notice
how you give of
yourself without
complaining.

Okay,
you complain
sometimes—

but you're
entitled.

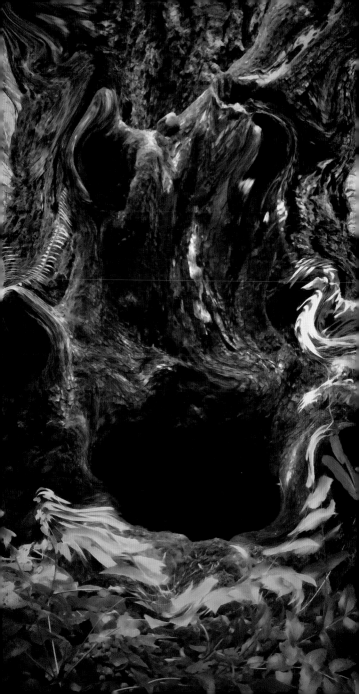

Y*our roots anchor you to*

the important things in life,

*and you don't let
the small stuff
get you down,*

which is a good thing,
considering all
the small stuff
I've brought your way.

Have I told you how much I've come to respect you?

I look up to you more than you know.

Dad, you stand tall.

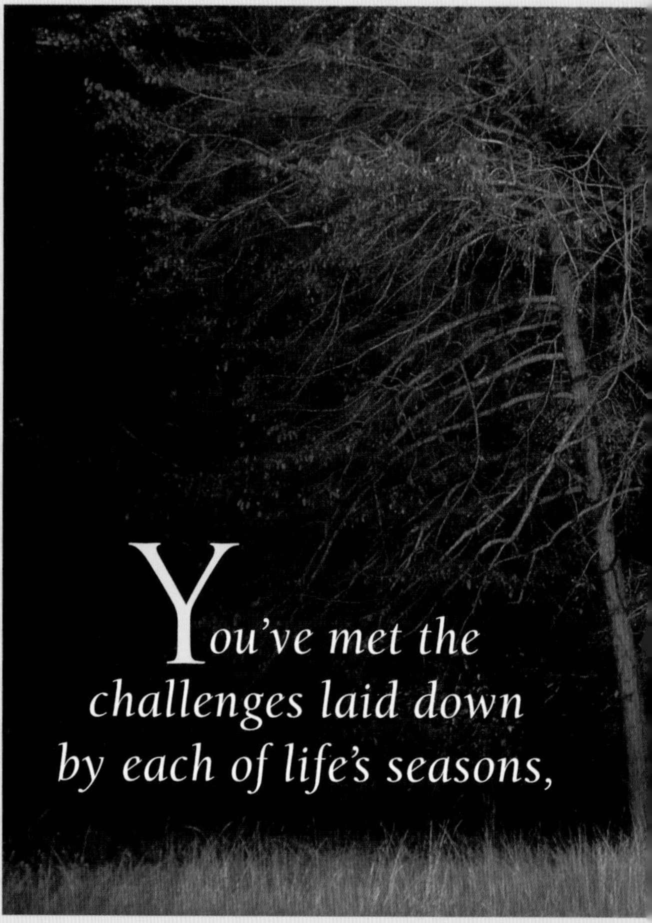

Y ou've met the
challenges laid down
by each of life's seasons,

and you're a winner.

You wear your rings
with dignity.

You can feel proud
of the man
looking back at you
in the mirror.

You've made an

impact on so many lives.

You're a provider . . .

and a protector.

You find strength
in solitude

and in friendship.

In your strength
and sharing,
you're an amazing
role model.

Dad, you stand tall.

I admit,
at times in my life
I've focused on
your imperfections.

Funny how
perceptions change.

*Now I see you
as the incredible
individual you are.*

With or without any hair.

Now I feel proud when people say

they see you in me.

Sure,

you're gnarly sometimes

*and a little
rough around
the edges.*

But I could never
question your heart.

I'm proud
to stand by you.

Dad, you stand tall.